A SUPERCHAM[P]

THE MEN OF THE HOUSE

For Nicola Cloughton

William Heinemann Ltd
Michelin House, 81 Fulham Road
London SW3 6RB

LONDON   MELBOURNE   AUCKLAND

First published 1990
Text © 1990 William Mayne
Illustrations © 1990 Michaela Stewart
ISBN 0 434 93085 7
Produced by Mandarin Offset
Printed in Hong Kong

A school pack of SUPERCHAMPS 7–12
is available from
Heinemann Educational Books
ISBN 0 435 00091 8

A SUPERCHAMP BOOK

THE MEN OF THE HOUSE

WILLIAM MAYNE

Illustrated by
MICHAELA STEWART

HEINEMANN · LONDON

Chapter 1

VISAP SENTA WAITED for the moon to turn into a new one. His two sisters waited as well. Panyap, their father, would return from his work in the forest when the moon was new again.

'Is he up there?' the sisters asked. 'In the top of that tree?' That was where they saw the moon, round as a golden melon. They thought their father might have walked there.

Visap tried how to explain that Panyap was in the forest, with the woodcutters, working to keep the land alive and green for the sake of everything that lived in it, telling the men which trees it was right to cut. When he had decided and the men had agreed, then he would walk home.

'He is not up there,' said Visap. 'He is a scientist for the government.'

'Then he cannot come back,' said the little sisters, not understanding his words at all. 'He cannot see us.' And they ran off to play in the yard.

'They do not know,' said Renidra, their mother, to Visap. 'But I wish they had not said it, because animals and young children often tell the future without knowing.'

'I shall look after you,' said Visap. 'I am the man of the house.' He thought that someone should be in charge.

Night by night the moon changed. The golden melon grew old and began to sag out of shape.

'It is being made new,' said Renidra. 'When it is ready to rise they will strike the gong at the temple.'

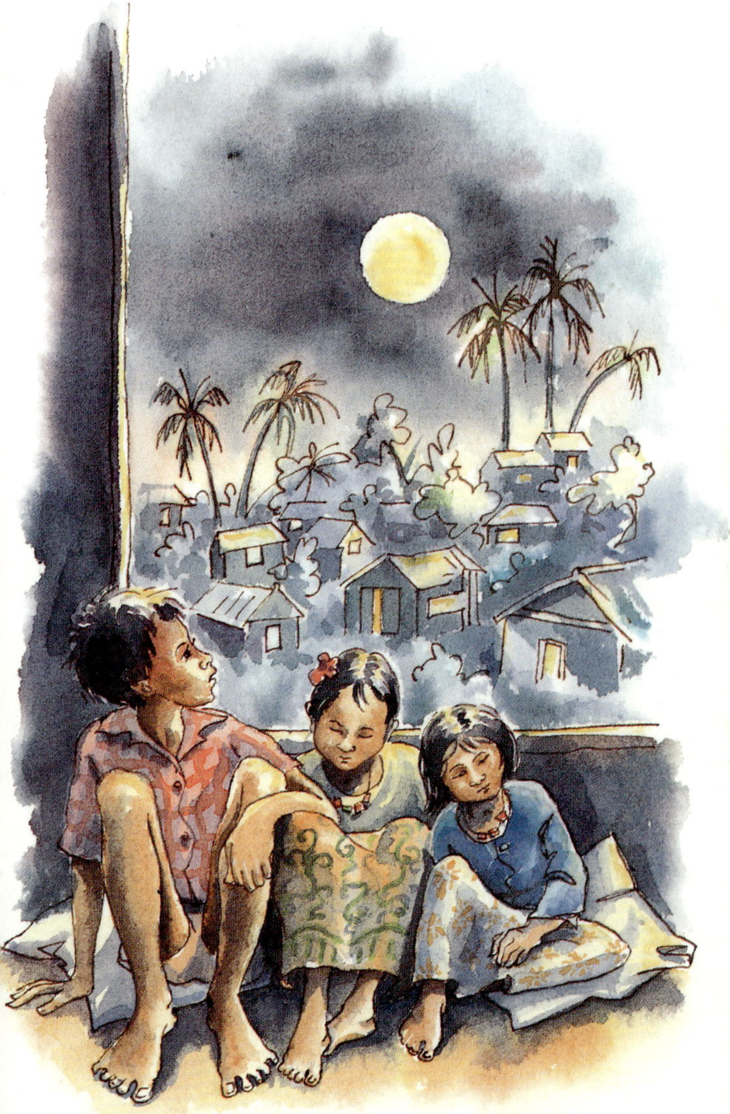

During that afternoon the temple gong made a great shivering sound across the village. This was the moment when the moon rose from the mountains, but darkness would come before it was high enough to see in the sky.

Renidra took Visap and the girls to the temple to pray in front of the table for a safe return for Panyap. The priests came out and sang. There were little fires in brass dishes and smoke with magic smells.

The old, old, temple monkey called Alakhap slept in his room in the wall, snoring gently. He wore a collar of braided gold wire. He sneezed at the scented smoke and put out his hand for food.

Visap's sisters looked at the old monkey. He had big eyes and a ruff of creamy white hair round his face.

He was the last of his breed, the priests said. Panyap, who was a scientist, said so too. He had persuaded the priests to take the lock from the door and let Alakhap close it himself if he wanted to be alone. Alakhap knew this and was grateful to Panyap. It was closed now. It was a cage door still, not a solid door, and Alakhap could be seen behind it.

'When he goes there will be a new monkey,' said the bigger sister solemnly, looking at Alakhap.

'Like the new moon,' said the smaller one.

Visap thought they might be telling the future about Alakhap, but must be wrong to say Panyap would not come back at the new moon. It was impossible to imagine that.

The sun went down. The sky turned dark. The stars came out and watched the village. Before long the new moon was hanging like a silver charm, fine and pointed, curved like a hook. It went up the sky, and up, and the stars near it faded.

'It is sliced up like a melon,' said the bigger sister.

'The seeds ran out,' said the other, looking at the stars.

Rice was laid out ready. There were small red fish from the market, meat was soaking in fruit and spices, three sauces and two pickles were ready, there was honey to eat when the meal was over. The fire had wood beside it, waiting to get to work.

They all waited, but Panyap did not come.

The little girls started dreaming, closed their eyes, rolled over on the floor, and had to be carried to bed.

'I do not think you will stay awake either,' said Renidra.

Visap was sure he would, but in the end he was dreaming without wanting to, and went to bed too. Only Renidra waited.

In the morning the rice was still

uncooked, the meat still soaking in its wooden bowl, the red fish still wrapped in their leaf, the sauces beginning to dry. Renidra sat by the fire. She had kept it alight all night, but Panyap had not come.

The house was empty because of that. Renidra went to the door and looked out again and again, but Panyap was never in the street. People walking there were never Panyap. They said 'Good morning,' but there was no news from Panyap. Later on they said 'Good afternoon,' but were not Panyap.

'The moon is still new,' said Renidra. The two little sisters sat by the fire and waited for Renidra to see them.

'I will cook,' she said. When she did, tears splashed in the embers of the fire. 'It is the smoke,' she said. 'He is never late.'

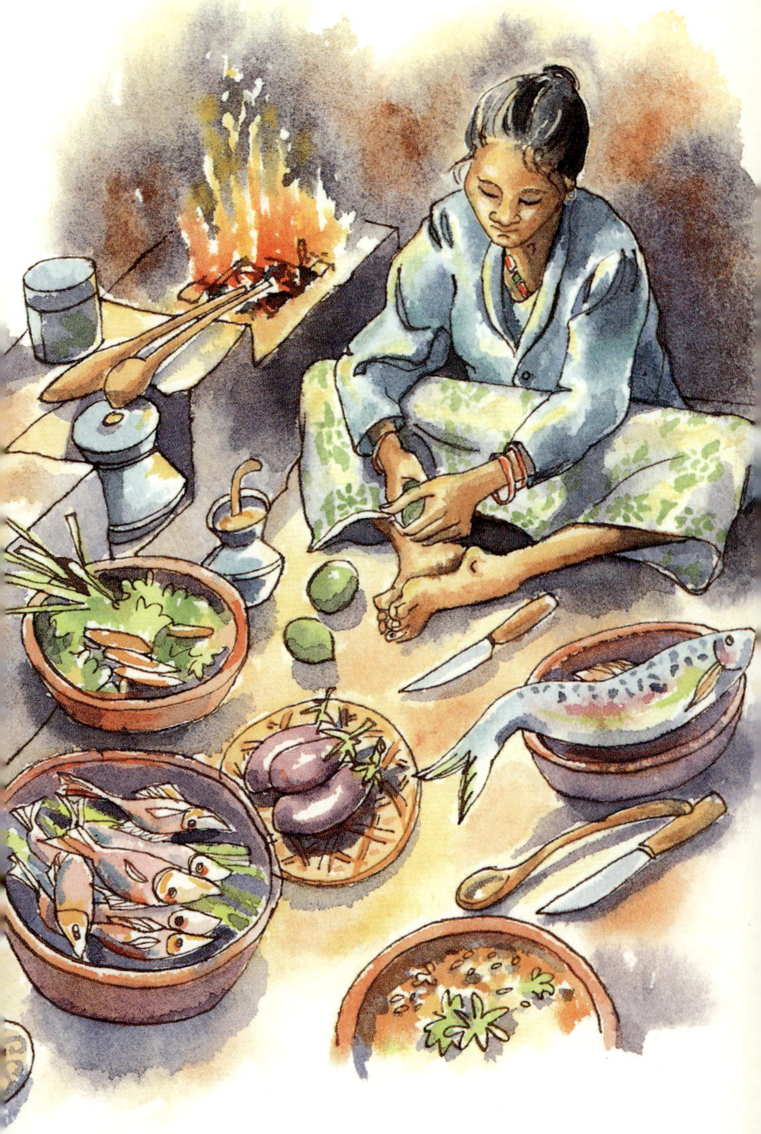

Visap did not know what to do in the house, or in the garden. The sunshine had become empty, and even the black and white birds quarrelling in the trees did not mean what they said.

The day ended worse than it began. At dusk a woodcutter came to the door with something soft in his hand. 'I found it in the forest three days ago as I came home,' he said. 'I think it is Panyap's blue head-cloth.'

Renidra took it and unrolled it. 'I stitched it myself.' Then her eyes jerked wide open and her throat said, 'Oh.' In the middle of the blue cloth there was a dark patch, dried stiff. Even in the dusk it showed redness.

'He will have cut himself,' said the man. 'Is he well?'

'He has not come back,' said Renidra. 'And you bring me his bloodstained head-cloth. What has happened?'

No one knew. A policeman came and said that they would look along the roads but could not search the forest. A neighbour came and looked after the little sisters.

Everyone thought about bandits without mentioning them.

The next night, too, Renidra did not sleep. She stayed by the fire and watched the moon travelling over the stars. Visap watched with her, sleeping and waking, not wanting to dream.

In the dark before dawn the moon was swept up by the trees. Renidra's eyes closed, whether she wanted them to or not. Visap sat with her for a time, and then could not bear to stay indoors. He slipped out at first light, wanting to be alone and away from the house.

He wondered whether he had prayed well the last time he was at the temple. He might have been too certain Panyap would return to bother what he thought or said. Now he went there to ask a priest. But there were no fires and no smoke and there was no priest in front of the table.

Only Alakhap, hunkered down in his room in the wall, watched with great eyes. He was listening to some far-off sound, and sniffing the air for a faint scent. His dark hand lay on the lowest bar of his door.

Visap went to speak to him. He held Alakhap's hand and thought about what he wanted to know, sure Alakhap was waiting to hear his prayer. Alakhap bent his head towards him and looked into his eyes. He lifted Visap's hand, and held it.

The monkey got up from his bed, undid the latch of the door, and pushed it open. He reached round the bars and brought Visap's hand along until the door was not between them. He held the hand firmly. It was clear he had something in mind.

He did not let go as he climbed down from his room. He took Visap to the table in the middle of the temple, and they both stood in front of it for a moment. They said their prayers together. Visap thought Alakhap did it better.

Alakhap turned away from the table and walked from the temple, taking Visap with him. They came out into the street.

'People will think I am stealing the temple monkey and his collar,' Visap thought. But no one was there to notice them.

Alakhap put an arm across Visap's shoulders, led him up through an alley, out of the village, and into the fields. He did not move quickly, but he neither let go nor did he hesitate.

Visap knew it must be all right, because this was the temple monkey himself, wiser than the priests. He was not stealing the temple monkey; the temple monkey was stealing him. He did not want to be stolen, and did not know why he should be.

After a time Alakhap looked into his eyes again and told him. The words were serious, but they were in monkey language. He held tighter and walked towards the distant forest, pointing ahead to it with his long arms. But was it right for Visap, good for the temple, or a bad monkey idea? Visap did not know what he ought to think, looking towards the forest or at Alakhap.

At home Renidra waited for the men of the house to return. The little girls brought flowers, but could not make her happy.

Chapter 2

THE PATH RAN straight, beside a straight water channel. The channel brought dark water to the fields. Yellow flowers with leaves like dishes grew in it. When the sun touched them croaking frogs took bubbling baths and sparkling showers. A black heron balanced exactly on the reflection of its yellow legs.

Alakhap walked with one arm on Visap's shoulders. His feet were slow, and his weight grew heavier and heavier.

'I must go home,' said Visap, stopping. He tried to take the great coil of arm from round his neck.

Alakhap kept hold, and walked on.

Visap struggled, becoming frightened. Even if he had a gold collar Alakhap was a large monkey, a wild animal of the forest. Something in the forest ate people from time to time.

The black heron fled the quarrel with clattering wings.

Alakhap sat down to examine one foot, where something hurt under his toes. He squashed Visap to him with his elbow and went on looking at his foot, making small noises of distress.

A hooked thorn had gone in, then twisted round. Alakhap was pulling it the wrong way. He sat sadly on the path, waiting to be made better. Visap took the thorn out. Alakhap said that the pain had been dreadful, and that he needed sympathy.

Visap's sisters would have been well again after a hug. So he hugged the hairy elbow that held him. Alakhap searched his head for him until Visap laughed with the tickling.

He was not allowed to go. Alakhap looked towards the far end of the path and started walking again. The path was very long, and the further they went the more distant the end was.

'I shall escape,' said Visap. Alakhap

probably said, 'We shall see,' but it was hard to tell.

A distant buzzing came from the village. Visap looked back. The buzzing became louder. He knew what made it before he saw a motor scooter between the fields and the water. It was bringing a farmer to work in his fields.

'I shall be rescued,' Visap told

Alakhap, sure that the farmer would stop and that Alakhap would run away. But Alakhap had lived beside a road far longer than Visap had, and was not disturbed by a motor scooter with three farmers on it, pulling a trailer full of hoes and sacks, bouncing along with tyres bulging and black smoke coming from its engine.

The exhaust pipe was broken and no farmer heard Visap call out that he was being stolen. Alakhap pulled him to one side to let the scooter pass. The farmers bowed, not to Visap but to Alakhap. The driver grinned, and the others were busy holding edges of scooter and corners of trailer.

The smoke and the noise rattled to the end of the path, turned right, and out of sight, then went out of hearing.

When Alakhap got to the end he was

only interested in going straight on. If the path would not do it, he would. Rows of beans grew across where he wanted to go, and he burst through sixteen of them like a machine. Visap thought that was very wrong.

A farmer heard the sticks breaking and came to deal with an animal spoiling crops, running with a rusty gun as long as himself, putting in gunpowder, ramming down bullets, cocking the hammer. He put the gun to his shoulder, aiming it. It pointed at everything in turn. Then he brought the gun down.

'He has seen me,' Visap thought. 'Help,' he shouted.

'Is it Alakhap?' the farmer called.

'Yes. Help,' Visap called back. 'He is taking me away.'

'I saw his collar,' the farmer replied.

'Why has he chosen you? What good thing have you done?'

'I want to go home,' Visap yelled.

The farmer waved and went away, unwilling to interfere.

Alakhap stopped in the next field, where sweetcorn grew in small and tender ears, and had breakfast. Alakhap ate whole heads. Visap chewed off the milky buds of grain.

Then there was sugar cane, with the stiff stems running their way. They had a meal here too. In the next crop Alakhap ate four small melons. They spent time cleaning each other up, yawning, closing their eyes and taking a rest. Alakhap never closed both eyes, and a hand was always near Visap.

After that, rice paddies made wide steps down the side of a valley. Alakhap did not want to get his feet wet. He had a good sniff and look towards the forest to get his direction, then walked the banks between the fields of water. He made Visap go in front, where he could see him. He went across, along, and down the slope. At the bottom a river lay brown and wide.

They came down to the water. Alakhap grunted and looked up and down. He sat and waited, calm, patient and knowing.

A boat went down the river on the far side, steam rising from it, no one looking their way as it rattled past.

A sailing boat came upwind in midstream, brave and silent like a natural thing, but no one saw Alakhap.

A little boat came along the bank below, with a fisherman in it prodding his way along with a pole, the oars lying with his lines and net among the fish he had caught.

'Hnggngh,' said Alakhap.

'Please help,' said Visap. All he had to do was jump in among the fish, push the boat out into the river, and be free.

'It is Alakhap,' said the fisherman, beaming and smiling. 'Alakhap is journeying.' He edged the boat in close.

Alakhap walked down and climbed aboard. He clambered to the front. Visap followed him on to the boat.

'I want to be rescued,' said Visap. 'He is taking me away.'

'If he is taking you, you are rescued already,' said the fisherman. 'Sit down. I will ferry you across the water.'

Visap turned away to climb back on to the bank.

'Keep still,' said the fisherman. And Alakhap reached out an arm longer than any he had had before, to dump

Visap down at the end of the boat.

'You see,' said the fisherman, 'he wishes to have you with him. Even I shall be blessed by lending him my boat.'

He took up his oars, dug his feet down among the fish, and began to row. The boat left the bank slowly.

Alakhap let go of Visap. On its way back to him his hand picked up the fisherman's hat and put it on his own head.

The fisherman repeated that carrying Alakhap was an undeserved honour. At the far side of the river he brought the boat in under an overhanging tree. Alakhap pulled himself on to the trunk. He gathered Visap up and put him on the ground.

The fisherman rowed away. Alakhap said things that made him release the oars and clasp his hands with delight.

Alakhap climbed the steep, wild bank, not holding Visap, yet not letting him out of sight. They ate berries from a bush. Alakhap ate leaves that tasted like rush matting to Visap.

Not far away there was the occasional noise of traffic on a road, trucks or motor bikes, or cars. Now and then the roar of a hooter was like the call of a forest creature.

'I shall stop a bus,' Visap thought. 'But I have no money. A car will take me home. There will be a policeman.'

It was not like that. They stood on the verge, hand in hand.

'It is safe to cross,' said Visap. He had some idea of seeing Alakhap across, then coming back and escaping. But Alakhap was not about to cross the road.

There was the grinding of gears. A wagon toiled along, heat rippling from the painted cab, dust swirling from the wheels.

Alakhap looked at it. Visap looked at Alakhap. 'Still time to get across,' he said, hoping that a trick would work. Alakhap showed his teeth. He put on the fisherman's hat.

'I am ashamed of you, dressed up

like that,' said Visap. 'You look silly.'
But it was not so, really. Alakhap was
like no one else and could not look
ridiculous. He was a holy monkey.

The holy monkey knew what he was
doing, as usual. He held up a large
hand, and began to hitch a lift.

The wagon slowed down and
stopped. Alakhap opened the door of
the cab and began to climb up.

'Alakhap,' said the driver. 'Do you want to take the wheel?'

'Please help me,' said Visap. 'I am being kidnapped.'

'Certainly,' said the driver. 'Where do you want to go, sir?'

'Home,' said Visap. But the driver was talking to Alakhap.

'Hgnung,' said Alakhap. It meant, 'Drive on. I will tell you when to stop.'

'It must be like a dream,' said the driver. 'I once had a share in the state lottery, but I'd rather be stolen by Alakhap any day. I know him by the collar, but I have no idea who you are.'

Visap told him. He told him about Renidra and the little sisters. He told him about Panyap and the new moon.

'They know you are safe with Alakhap,' said the driver.

'They do not know where I am at all,' said Visap. 'It is my fault for not praying well enough, I am sure.' His eyes felt hot, and there were tears running down his cheeks.

'You are lucky,' said the driver, switching on his headlamps.

Alakhap scratched Visap's head again, until it was too dark to see anything. Visap curled against the seat, between Alakhap and the shrugging cover of the engine, and went to sleep. He last saw Alakhap looking at the dusk outside.

Then Alakhap had told the driver to stop. He woke Visap, opened the door, and climbed down past the front wheel and the hissing brake. For thanks he put the fisherman's hat on the driver's head. The wagon rolled on, hooting goodbye, gears snarling, red lamps winking good night.

They were in the forest. It stretched away on either side, wild and unknown. Alakhap breathed in its smell, took Visap's hand, and led him into the dark depths.

Far down the road the wagon sounded its siren again. Away in the forest something honked under the trees.

Chapter 3

THE NEW MOON climbed high among wisps of cloud. Shadows flew black against it. Stealthy rustlings filled the forest. Visap was shivering, hungry, homesick, alone.

Alakhap pushed him on, eating leaves. He gave Visap handfuls, but they were too hard to bite. Visap remembered red fish, rice, meat soaked in fruit and spices, forest honey.

Alakhap belched when he had eaten enough, but went on tearing down small branches. He tucked a bundle under one arm, spoke a few words to Visap, and disappeared. He had been difficult to see in the shadows. Now he had gone utterly.

Twigs and leaves fell on Visap's head. A tree creaked and shook. Alakhap had climbed it to make a nest for the night, and his untidy bedmaking scattered the litter he had carried up. He wanted Visap to follow him to the nest like a good child. He chided for some time, but Visap could not climb in the dark. Alakhap rebuilt his bed lower down the tree.

'The panthers will get me,' he probably said.

'I don't care,' Visap said aloud. But he did not want to be taken by panthers either, and his voice was quiet.

Alakhap settled himself just overhead. Visap pushed himself among the roots of the tree and listened for panthers.

In the very early morning Alakhap was snoring loudly. The moon was low in the trees. Visap thought he could run back to the road. He crawled from his rooty corner, then tip-toed stiffly away, Alakhap snoring on quite undisturbed.

'I've done it,' thought Visap, making not a sound. Alakhap reached down an arm and pulled him back to the tree, still snoring. His mouth said, 'Chack, chack, chack,' in his sleep.

'Sorry,' said Visap, pushed into the corner again. The hand scratched his head. Snoring continued.

Later on the forest was full of light at the ground and shadow at the top. Alakhap was awake and eating again. 'Have some breakfast,' he said cheerily, waving leaves. But there was nothing Visap dared eat. Alakhap ate them.

'I'm going home,' said Visap. 'I am.' He was not. When he turned away, one long dark finger hooked into the waistband of his trousers, and that was that. 'I know how to get back to the road,' said Visap. 'I shall go. I am not lucky to be with you. It is the worst thing that ever happened to me. I want to go home,' he shouted.

Alakhap showed his teeth and shouted back. Visap sulked and walked away. Alakhap ran up a tree, swung to the next, hung from a low branch, and picked Visap up.

His arms were much stronger than his legs. He was a slow walker but fast among the branches. Even with Visap's weight doubling his, he went faster than Visap could walk.

He had been in the temple for years, without forgetting branches. Visap was terrified and shut his eyes, expecting to have his brains dashed out. When he was not dropped from the first tree, he expected to fall from the next. Alakhap hitched him closer, but Visap became unfastened.

He found himself falling through branches alone, with Alakhap in mid-jump able to do nothing until he landed. Then a long arm raked Visap from the air, somersaulted him, and put him firmly in the cleft of a tree, breathless. He put his arms round the tree trunk and wanted never to move again.

The tree thinned away below him without another branch. He saw the ground further away than he could imagine, distant and unreal. Alakhap sat in another tree, scolding him. Visap cried to his tree, and it took no notice. He thought of his bones sitting here for ever in his shirt and trousers.

The tree rocked. Alakhap had landed behind him, and was pulling to get him from his place. Moving was worse than staying, but the long arms were stronger than his short ones. They plucked him into the air again, going from arm to hairy arm as he and Alakhap fell headlong.

Alakhap had him the right way round. They swung up, then down, and Visap lay on the earth holding a thorny bush.

'I shall walk,' he told Alakhap. 'But why can't I go home?'

Alakhap had no answer. Visap stood up at last. He held his trousers up because the waistband had been torn through.

Alakhap laughed at him. 'It is fair,' said Visap, remembering Alakhap in the fisherman's hat. 'I have laughed at you.'

They went on, Alakhap swaying through the trees, Visap walking and

holding himself together. Then
Alakhap halted, sniffing, showing his
teeth, making small noises.

Visap smelt the woodsmoke before
long. A band of men had lit a fire to
cook a meal. Visap smelt meat roasting,
bread baking. Alakhap tried to stop him
going to the men, swinging down to
pick up him. Visap tripped over his
trousers, and the long arm missed him.
Alakhap yipped angrily.

Visap got up, clutched his waistband,
and ran towards the fire, shouting for
help. The men by the fire turned
round, and Visap saw what they had in
their hands. They were armed with
swords and daggers and spears. Visap
had run into a camp of forest bandits,
who lived as outlaws. No one returned
from meeting them.

'Who is with you?' shouted one with

a silver gun. 'Go and search, some of you. How many more?'

'Slit him up,' said a bandit with a crooked sword. 'Roast him on the fire. We can eat children.'

Visap knew that was only true about naughty children. 'I want to be rescued,' he said. 'I haven't done anything wrong.'

'The mistake of finding us is bad

enough,' said the leader with the gun. 'Who else is with you? Speak the truth.'

'Nobody,' said Visap. 'I was stolen by a monkey.'

'He's telling lies,' said crooked sword. 'We'll deal with him.'

The leader was looking round. 'Not so fast,' he said. 'There's a monkey up there in that kapok tree.'

'I'll use a bow and arrow,' said crooked sword. 'It'll roast.'

'It's wearing a collar,' said the leader. 'A gold one.'

'It's Alakhap,' said Visap. 'I was telling you. But I want to go home.' His insides squealed with hunger. What he needed was a huge drink and a huge meal. He could be roasted later.

The leader told him to be quiet. To the bandits he said, 'Put down your weapons. It is Alakhap up there. He is journeying.'

The bandits put down their swords. Visap did not know it, but such a thing never happened. They bowed to Alakhap, pleased to see him. Outlaws do not expect holy monkeys.

Alakhap came down. The bandits let him walk to Visap to take him away, but begged him to stay. They said it in words. They brought fruit and heaped it at his feet. 'We shall all come with you,' they said. 'Tell us what to do.' They held his hands.

Alakhap wanted Visap. He wanted the fruit as well, and stayed to eat it. Visap too was waited on by bandits, brought roast meat and bread, and a sweet drink. Before Alakhap took him, the leader gave Visap his own belt to hold up his trousers.

'I shall leave it in the yard of Panyap's house if I get home,' he said. 'My father is Panyap. Have you seen him?'

The bandits had heard of him. 'If we see him we shall say Alakhap needed you,' said crooked sword. 'He will be pleased about that. Perhaps you are not?'

'I am not,' said Visap. 'But I do not know the words to use.'

'You do not know the sense,' said the leader. 'If you knew the sense the words would not matter.'

Alakhap left now, dragging Visap away, one finger in the new belt. They walked through the forest with night falling. Then there was only sky ahead, bright with a rising moon, three days old and fatter. The trees had stopped and the ground had been cut off, sliced away.

They were at the top of a high cliff.
Alakhap went to the edge, and brought
Visap with him. They looked over and
heard a mighty river swirling far below.

Alakhap swung himself over the
edge. He pulled Visap down where he
would not dare go alone, to a shelf on
the cliff-face. Then he led him down
and down in the moonlight.

And Visap thought he had come home. He saw the pointed ridges of a temple roof, close under the cliff. There were priests in the temple, praying in front of the table, taking part in ceremonies. The temple was the one he knew, but shadowy in moonlight, like a dream. Alakhap walked into it and climbed into his own room. Visap had no idea where he was.

Chapter 4

Visap sat down against the cliff, and did not know what to think. His mind was too weary to understand. No one took any notice of him.

This was a temple, full of priests and people. There was some strange difference about it, but when he tried to think about it he fell asleep and stopped dreaming.

When he woke, the crescent of the moon had shot high up the sky and was burning into his eyes. He was too dazzled to see who had roused him by bringing a bowl of rice. A priest must have brought it, but he wished it had been Renidra, or Panyap. The rice was cold but good. He fell asleep again.

When he woke, daylight was round him. The priests and worshippers had gone away. He was alone beside a temple in a cliff that went straight down to misty river below, and straight up to misty forest above.

Alakhap came out of the mist and looked at Visap from the far side of the temple. It could be no other monkey with the creamy white ruff, because Alakhap was the last of his kind. All the same, Visap was not sure because he did not see the gold-braided collar.

Alakhap, his own self with the golden collar, climbed down from his room and sat on the cliff edge. Visap knew the monkey he had seen before was not Alakhap, and that Alakhap was not the last of his kind. 'I shall tell them,' he thought. 'I shall tell Panyap.' He waited for Alakhap to speak.

Something came rolling and squealing across the temple floor. It burst apart, and was two very small monkeys playing at a fight, their ruffs spread out in disarray, their tails and arms and legs entangled with themselves and each other.

They saw Visap and leapt away, jumping straight on to the back and side of Alakhap. They were of his kind.

He held them, stroking their heads, talking to them, soothing them. They rolled their eyes at Visap.

Their mother came down from the cliff above, long-armed, slim and graceful, and stood on all fours beside Alakhap. He greeted her lips with a kiss from his lips. She took her children from him and went out beyond the temple.

Alakhap stretched out an arm to Visap. It was an order to come to him. They sat together. There was no kiss. Alakhap put an arm across Visap's shoulders and took him past the temple. There, sitting on the rocks in the sun, were the priests and worshippers Visap had seen in moonlight the night before.

They were monkeys of Alakhap's kind, twenty or thirty of them, large and small. None were so old as Alakhap.

Alakhap spoke. They replied. One of them went to fetch the bowl that had held rice. Last night Visap had thought the monkeys were priests, and now he saw they were not. But monkeys do not cook rice and put it in bowls, so there was something strange here.

What he found was stranger than he thought, though it was something he had had in mind for days.

Sitting on a monkeys' nest in the middle of the group was a man in a blue shirt. For some reason he had leaves tied to his head, and held it, as if it hurt. For some other reason that Visap did not know, the man was Panyap. Visap went slowly to greet him. He knew it was true, but could not believe it.

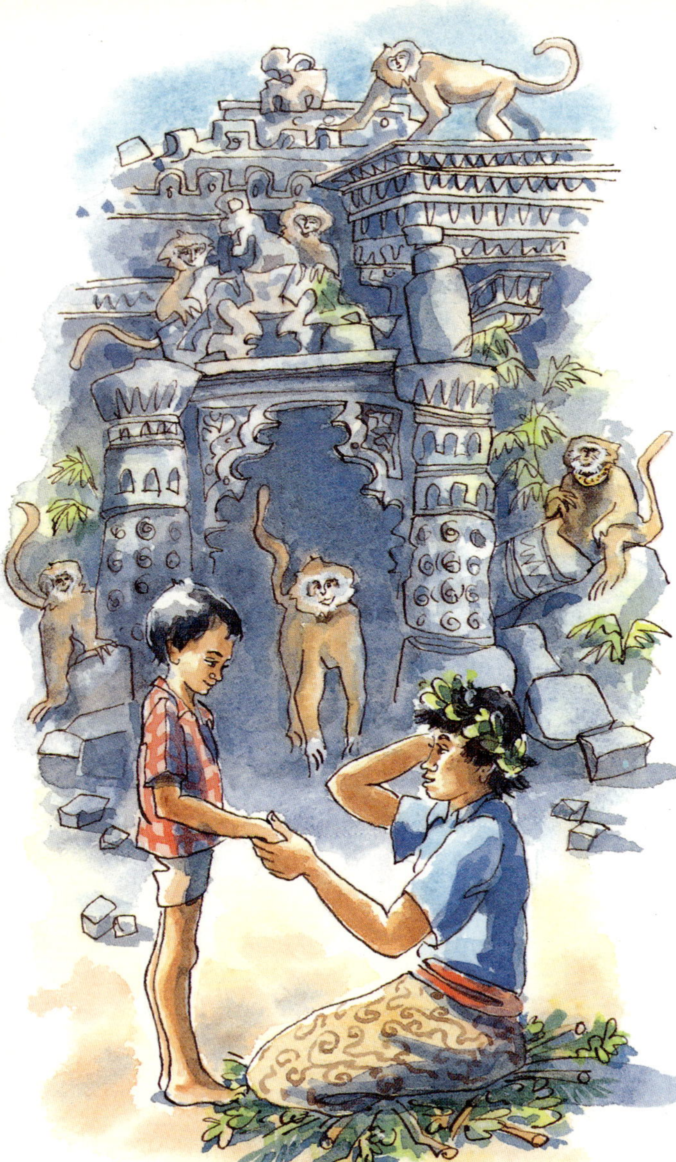

A monkey chittered at him, showing its teeth, being alarmed. Panyap looked up, slowly. The monkey held on to its friend and pretended it had not spoken.

Panyap looked round at all the monkeys. His eyes went past Visap, then swivelled back to him. He tried to get up, but seemed too dizzy. Visap went to him and stood there, not sure what to do or how to help. He held Panyap's hand. It was cold.

'I know you are only a vision,' said Panyap. 'I am grateful for that. Look after your mother and your sisters, and be the man of the house, just as these monkeys are the men of the temple.'

'I am real,' said Visap. 'I do not know about you. I walked here with Alakhap. He brought me to you.' Because it was clear now that it was so, but had not been clear before. He had indeed been fortunate to be stolen by Alakhap.

Panyap looked round the group. His head still hurt him, and his eyes saw with difficulty. 'I see the collar,' he said. 'Alakhap knew that I was here and also that he must find another temple monkey. They are wiser than men and were priests before men were.'

They sat in silence for a while, Panyap feeling very dizzy, Visap feeling both happy and unhappy. 'I was walking through the forest,' said Panyap. 'Coming home. I saw a monkey of Alakhap's kind and followed it. I did not believe it. If it was true the scientific interest would be very great. But when we were different ends of a tree trunk, the cliff-top gave way. I have not yet tried to find a way out because my head still hurts me. The monkeys have understood that I am in the grounds of their temple. They have been priests here for thousands of years.'

'I have eaten your rice,' said Visap, feeling guilty.

'You shall cook me some more at home,' said Panyap. 'But first Alakhap has something to say.'

Alakhap was busy with his collar, trying to take it off.

'There is a screwdriver in my pack,' said Panyap. 'I always carry it. You must put it through a hole in the collar and take it apart easily. You will see. I have done it at the temple in the village when it had to be mended.'

Alakhap sat still while Visap undid the three screws that held the collar together. Alakhap drew it from his neck and held it up. It kept its shape and was slightly flexible. Alakhap scratched his neck. He reached the long arm out and pulled another monkey towards him.

It came forward willingly to Alakhap, but was wary of Visap. Alakhap held Visap and the collar with one hand, the shy monkey with the other, and drew them closer.

Visap saw the monkey trembling, but brave; he shook a little himself, with shyness.

'Alakhap is sending another to take his place in the temple,' said Panyap.

With his own dark hands Alakhap put the collar round the other's neck. Visap screwed the screws in place. The new temple monkey felt the collar, and went to sit apart from the others for a time to get used to the idea. He turned it round. He scratched at it with his hand, then with his foot. He stood on his head to shake it off over his ruff. Alakhap had had a few words with him and he came to sit near Visap.

When the moon was full again Panyap was well and wanted to leave. An escort of monkeys came with Panyap and Visap through the forest, to the road. It took them two days, because Panyap was still dizzy. The new temple monkey walked hand in hand with Visap, sometimes happily, sometimes mournfully.

Then Visap, Panyap, and the new Alakhap were standing by the road, waiting for the right thing to happen. A wagon, the same wagon, stopped beside them. Visap opened the door.

'Have you been waiting long, sir?' asked the driver. He was talking to the new Alakhap. 'Just remember I come up and down each week. You'll want your hat back.'

'It is strange,' said Visap, when they got off by the river. But many years later he knew it was not, when he learnt that strange things are the real ones.

'It is Alakhap,' said Panyap.

The fisherman was at the river bank. 'We are servants,' he said, putting on his hat. 'My whole life was for this one task.'

When evening prayers began in the temple, with priests singing and smoke rising, the new Alakhap went to his room in the wall and opened the door. He threw out three cushions, a bundle of firewood, and a cat. The singing stopped and the priests watched.

Alakhap looked inside, came out, and went to the table to pray. The priests began again with him.

'Stay here,' said Panyap to Visap. He went for Renidra and the little girls. All the family came to be thankful.

Said the chief of the priests, taking Visap's face and looking into his eyes, 'Alakhap has chosen you. When you are twelve, you will come to the temple and enter the company of priests.'

'Yes,' said Visap. He understood that Alakhap knew.

The new Alakhap howled. 'That is worship,' said the priests. 'It is his destiny to be a man of the house.'

'We thought so,' said the little sisters, wiser even than monkeys.

A SUPERCHAMP BOOK

Helen Cresswell
ROSIE AND THE
BOREDOM EATER
0 434 93061 X

Gwen Grant
THE WALLOPING
STICK WAR
0 434 93055 5

Michael Hardcastle
MARK ENGLAND'S CAP
0 434 93065 2

Carmen Harris
NAOMI'S SECRET
0 434 93107 1

Mary Hoffman
DOG POWDER
0 434 93059 8

Robert Leeson
HOW ALICE SAVED
CAPTAIN MIRACLE
0 434 93063 6

Sam McBratney
THE THURSDAY
CREATURE
0 434 93089 X